THE MILLIONAIRE MINDSET

Cracking the Code of
Success, Money, and
Contentment
By
Israel Daniel

Disclaimer

Table of contents

Introduction

For many years, the idea of the "millionaire mindset" has captured the interest of individuals all around the world. It is thought to represent a collection of values, attitudes, and behaviors that are essential to prosperity and prosperity in terms of money. However, what precisely is a millionaire's thinking, and how is it different from the ordinary person's mindset? In this overview, we will investigate the underlying ideas of the millionaire mindset, look at some of its salient features, and consider how adopting this mindset might lead to both financial success and personal contentment.

The millionaire mindset is fundamentally an abundance mindset as opposed to a scarcity mindset. It is defined by the conviction that everyone, from any background or situation, can build wealth and succeed financially. People with a millionaire mindset see opportunities everywhere and think that success can be attained through hard work, perseverance, and determination, in contrast to many others who operate from

a mindset of scarcity, believing that there is only a limited amount of wealth to go around and that success has been reserved for the lucky few. Strong confidence and self-belief are essential elements of the millionaire mindset. Millionaires have faith in their own abilities to succeed and believe that they can overcome any obstacle. They know exactly what they want to achieve and are prepared to take chances and give up things in order to make their goals come true. Their activities are motivated by this unrelenting self-confidence, which pushes them to step beyond of their comfort zones and pursue their objectives with fervor and conviction.
A concentration on development and ongoing education is another characteristic of the millionaire mindset. Millionaires are dedicated to lifelong learning and personal development because they recognize that

success is a journey rather than a destination. They read a lot and are always looking for new concepts, viewpoints, and methods to broaden their knowledge and abilities. They also welcome criticism and comments, seeing failure and setbacks as chances for improvement and education rather than as reasons to give up.

The millionaire mindset is defined by a strong work ethic and a willingness to take initiative in addition to self-belief and ongoing learning. Millionaires are aware that hard effort, perseverance, and dedication are necessary for success and that it does not come easily. Even if it requires making compromises or overcoming challenges along the road, they are prepared to invest the time and energy required to accomplish their objectives. Even though they are aware that failure and success are inevitable parts of the road, they are unfazed by setbacks and keep their eyes on the prize—the long term picture.

The millionaire mindset is also distinguished by its emphasis on thankfulness and wealth. Millionaires know that having riches is about living a full and meaningful life rather than just having money. They approach life with a sense of abundance, appreciating what they already have and the limitless opportunities and possibilities that lie ahead of them. They believe that the more they give, the more they will receive, thus they are giving freely of their time, money, and knowledge.

In summary, the millionaire mindset is an effective way of thinking that has the capacity to change a person's entire life, not just their financial circumstances. It is defined by an appreciation for life, self-assurance, hard effort, constant learning, and abundance. Anyone can realize their full potential and build a prosperous, successful, and fulfilling life by embracing the millionaire mindset and these fundamental values. We will go deeper into these ideas in this book and offer doable tactics and methods for developing the billionaire mindset in your own life.

You'll learn how to:

Develop an optimistic and abundant outlook.

Overcome self-doubt and limiting beliefs.

Set and accomplish bold objectives

Gain resiliency and tenacity in the face of hardship.

Learn the fundamentals of creating wealth and managing money.

Cultivate deep connections and harness the potential of teamwork.

Contribute to the betterment of others and the world.

"The Millionaire Mindset" has something to offer everyone, whether they are seasoned professionals, aspiring entrepreneurs, or just someone who wants to reach their full potential and live a life of wealth. So, are you prepared to set off on this adventure and discover the keys to a prosperous life? If so, let's get started and investigate the millionaire mindset.

The Influence of Mentality

The importance of mentality in achieving prosperity and success cannot be emphasized. Our ideas, habits, and results are greatly influenced by our mindset, which is the way we view the world, ourselves, and our capabilities. According to the millionaire mindset, success and the creation of an abundant and fulfilling life depend on developing an optimistic and empowered mindset. We will examine the essential ideas, methods, and approaches that enable people to change their viewpoint and maximize the power of their mindset for achievement in

this thorough examination of
the billionaire mindset.

Recognizing the Influence of Mentality

Fundamentally, mentality
describes the attitudes,
presumptions, and beliefs that
influence how we view the
world and ourselves. Our
mentality affects how we see
the world, how we decide what
to do, and how we react to
opportunities and obstacles.
According to the millionaire
mindset, a person's thinking
has the capacity to either help
them achieve their goals or
prevent them from realizing
their greatest potential.
A fixed mindset and a
development mindset are the
two main mindset types that
people might have. The idea
that our skills and aptitudes are
unchangeable, fixed
characteristics that cannot be
improved upon is the hallmark
of a fixed mindset. People with
a fixed attitude are more likely

to shy away from obstacles, give up easily when things don't go their way, and believe that work is in vain. Conversely, a growth mindset is defined by the conviction that our skills and aptitudes may be enhanced with commitment and diligence. People that have a growth mentality welcome challenges, keep going after failures, and see effort as a means of reaching success and mastery.

The Effect of Success on Mentality

The potential of our attitude to influence our ideas, actions, and results is what gives it its power. Our mentality affects how we view chances and difficulties, how we handle setbacks and disappointments, and ultimately, how successful we are in realizing our dreams. According to the millionaire mindset, success is mostly determined by one's mindset. Millionaires are aware that their thoughts greatly influence the world in which they live, and that by developing an optimistic and empowering outlook, they can surmount challenges, realize their objectives, and build a prosperous and fulfilling existence.

Furthermore, studies have demonstrated that growth-minded people are more successful, resilient, and adaptive than fixed-minded people. They are more capable of overcoming obstacles, learning from mistakes, and recovering from setbacks. People can realize their full potential and experience more success and fulfillment in all facets of their lives by embracing a growth mindset.

Techniques for Changing Your Mentality for Success

Intentional work and practice are necessary to change your thinking for success. Thankfully, there are a number of techniques people can employ to develop an optimistic and powerful mindset:

1. Develop self-awareness by becoming conscious of the attitudes, ideas, and perceptions you have about your skills and abilities. Take note of any limiting ideas or negative self-talk that might be preventing you from realizing your full potential. Substitute these misconceptions with empowering ideas and positive affirmations that can help you succeed and flourish.

2. Develop a growth mindset by accepting the idea that your skills and abilities can be improved with commitment and effort. Accept obstacles as chances for development and education, and see failure as a necessary component of learning. Honor your development and achievements while acknowledging that hard work and persistence are essential components of success.

3. Concentrate on the here and now: Pay attention to the here and now to cultivate awareness and presence. Give up worrying about the past and the future and give your all to the duties and activities at hand. You may improve your efficacy and productivity, lessen stress and anxiety, and develop a stronger sense of calm and wellbeing by keeping your attention in the here and now.

4. Establish objectives and act: Specify objectives that are in line with your beliefs, interests, and aspirations. Divide more ambitious objectives into more doable tasks and phases, then take persistent, targeted effort to accomplish them. Acknowledge and appreciate each little accomplishment along the path, and turn setbacks into teaching moments.

5. Develop an attitude of thankfulness: Show appreciation for all the

possibilities and gifts in your life. Every day, set aside some time to consider your blessings, whether they are related to your accomplishments, relationships, or well-being. By engaging in thankfulness practices, you can change your perspective from one of scarcity to one of abundance and develop a more fulfilled and contented feeling.

6. Embrace positivity: Surround yourself with people who make you feel good about yourself, such as encouraging friends, mentors, and role models who exhibit the attitudes and ideals of success. Reduce your exposure to harmful influences including toxic people, the media, and places that propagate negativity or constricting ideas.

The Millionaire Mindset's Role of Mentality

According to the millionaire mindset, a person's thinking has the capacity to either help them achieve their goals or prevent them from realizing their greatest potential. Millionaires are aware that their thoughts greatly influence the world in which they live, and that by developing an optimistic and empowering outlook, they can surmount challenges, realize their objectives, and build a prosperous and fulfilling existence.

Furthermore, success in the business and entrepreneurial worlds is heavily influenced by one's thinking. Growth-minded entrepreneurs are better equipped to deal with change, welcome ambiguity, and persevere in the face of difficulties. They are more likely to accomplish their objectives and produce long-lasting success when they approach their work with optimism, creativity, and resilience.

The millionaire mindset proves beyond a doubt the impact of mindset. A positive and empowered mindset can help people overcome challenges, accomplish their objectives, and build an abundant and fulfilling life. People can change their perspective to one of success, view obstacles as chances for personal development, and realize their full potential in all facets of their lives with deliberate practice and effort. Are you prepared to use your thoughts to their full potential and design the life you have always wanted? The voyage has begun.

Developing a Wealth Mentality

Building a wealth mindset is crucial to achieving prosperity and financial success. A wealth mindset is a collection of ideas, routines, and dispositions that enable people to build wealth, attain financial independence, and have abundant and satisfying lives. It transcends the simple act of accumulating wealth. This in-depth examination of developing a wealth mindset within the framework of the millionaire mindset will cover the essential ideas, tactics, and methods that enable people to change their perspective and welcome abundance in all facets of their lives.

Recognizing the Wealth Mindset

The foundation of the wealth mindset is a conviction in opportunity, possibility, and abundance. People who have a wealth mindset see the world as abundant rather than scarcity, believing that there is more than enough money and resources for everyone. They go into life with confidence, optimism, and a sense of possibilities because they think they deserve success and riches.

Moreover, a dedication to development, education, and self-improvement characterizes the wealth mindset. People with a wealth mindset devote time, effort, and resources to increasing their knowledge, skills, and talents because they recognize that it is crucial for both professional and personal growth.

The Wealth Mindset's Attitudes, Habits, and Beliefs

Developing a wealth mindset entails embracing particular attitudes, behaviors, and beliefs that promote prosperity and success. Among them are:

1. Belief in abundance: Adopt the mindset that there is more than sufficient money and resources for everyone. Develop an attitude of gratitude for the chances and

benefits in your life and embrace an abundance mindset that sees development and prosperity in every circumstance.

2. Positive self-talk: Pay attention to your inner monologue and swap out negative thoughts and affirmations with empowered ones. Develop a mindset of self-assurance, resiliency, and self-belief by engaging in self-love, self-compassion, and self-acceptance practices.

3. Establish definite, well-defined objectives that are consistent with your beliefs, interests, and aspirations. Divide more ambitious objectives into more doable tasks and phases, then take persistent, targeted effort to accomplish them. Acknowledge and appreciate each little accomplishment along the path, and turn setbacks into teaching moments.

4. Learn about investment, wealth-building tactics, and

personal finance to become financially literate. Gain a thorough understanding of money management concepts and establish investing, saving, and budgeting practices that will promote long-term financial security and success.

5. Taking risks: Accept risk as an inherent component of the process of accumulating wealth. In order to achieve your objectives and aspirations, be willing to push yourself beyond your comfort zone and take calculated risks, knowing that there is a chance for return. Use setbacks and failures as teaching moments to improve your methods and strategies.

6. Gratitude: Develop an attitude of thankfulness for all of life's blessings and plenty. Instead of concentrating on lack or scarcity, practice appreciation rituals like writing, meditation, or daily affirmations. You can also try journaling.

7. Generosity: Give back to others and further the common good by engaging in acts of generosity and philanthropy. Give to people in need of your resources (money, time, and skills) and improve the lives of others by doing deeds of kindness, compassion, and service.

Techniques for Fostering an Wealth Mindset

A wealth mindset must be intentionally developed through practice and effort. Thankfully, people can adopt a number of techniques to change their perspective and welcome wealth in all facets of their lives:

1. Visualization: Make use of this technique to see yourself leading the life you've always wanted. Imagine yourself reaching your objectives, being financially independent, and leading a prosperous and contented life. You may rewire your subconscious mind to

believe that you can accomplish your objectives and draw prosperity into your life by picturing success.

2. Affirmations: Rewire your subconscious mind with empowering attitudes and ideas by using positive affirmations. You can strengthen your confidence, self-belief, and sense of worthiness by repeatedly repeating statements such as I am capable of achievement and abundance, I attract prosperity and wealth into my life, and I am capable of accomplishing my goals and aspirations.

3. Encircle yourself with positive influences: Assemble a network of friends, mentors, and role models who share the beliefs and principles of the wealth mindset. Reduce your exposure to harmful influences such unhealthy relationships, the media, and places that promote lack or scarcity.

4. Lifelong learning: Make a commitment to your own

personal growth and ongoing education. Through books, courses, seminars, and workshops, devote time, effort, and resources to enhancing your knowledge, skills, and abilities. Continue to be inquisitive, flexible, and open-minded, and welcome fresh chances for development and education in all facets of your life.

5. Take inspired action: Make steady, deliberate progress toward your objectives. Define your bigger objectives, break them down into smaller, more doable tasks and action stages, and make conscious daily progress toward your goals. Be open to stepping beyond of your comfort zone in order to pursue possibilities for growth and expansion, and have faith in your inner direction and intuition.

6. Develop tenacity and resilience in the face of obstacles and setbacks by practicing resilience. Consider challenges as chances for

development and education, and even during trying times, keep an optimistic outlook. To overcome challenges and succeed, stay committed to your aims and objectives and be flexible in modifying your approach as necessary.

The Millionaire Mindset's Use of Wealth Mindset Cultivation

Building a wealth mindset is not just a goal for personal growth in the millionaire mindset; it is a fundamental idea that guides the entire success philosophy. People can cultivate a success mindset and realize their financial ambitions by embracing ideas, routines, and attitudes that promote wealth and plenty. Furthermore, developing a wealth mindset enables people to design a fulfilling life that is abundant in all respects other than money. People can draw opportunities, resources, and experiences that promote their development, prosperity, and happiness by adopting an abundance mindset in their thoughts, beliefs, and deeds. To succeed and experience abundance in the millionaire mindset, one must cultivate a wealth mindset. People can cultivate a success mindset and draw chances and wealth into their lives by embracing ideas, routines, and attitudes that promote prosperity and abundance.

People may embrace plenty in all facets of their lives—from their relationships and personal development to their work and finances—by making a conscious effort and practicing it. People can create a life of richness, meaning, and fulfillment that transcends monetary wealth by developing a wealth mindset. Are you prepared to change your perspective and welcome plenty in every aspect of your life? The voyage has begun.

Establishing Objectives and Acting

A fundamental component of the millionaire mindset is the pursuit of wealth and financial prosperity through the creation of specific objectives and the implementation of decisive action. People can make a successful strategy and reach their financial goals by setting clear goals and putting smart plans into action. We will dive into the core ideas, methods, and strategies that enable people to build wealth and attain financial freedom in this in-depth examination of goal-setting and acting within the billionaire mindset.

Realizing How Important Goal-Setting Is

According to the millionaire mindset, setting goals is the first step towards creating money. A person's actions and decisions are guided by their goals, which give them a clear purpose and direction and help them achieve particular results. People can increase their chances of success by more effectively focusing their time and resources by clearly outlining their goals and setting quantifiable targets. Additionally, goal-setting assists people in defining their beliefs, priorities, and goals so that their actions are in line with their long-term success vision. People can maintain their motivation and commitment to taking persistent action towards their financial and personal objectives by defining meaningful goals that are relevant to them.

Essential Guidelines for Setting Effective Goals

A few fundamental ideas underpin successful goal-setting in the millionaire mindset:

1. Specificity: Individuals should clearly state their goals and indicate when they wish to reach them. Goals should be well-defined, precise, and obvious. Having clear and specific goals makes it easier for people to stay on course and track their progress.

2. Measurability: Objectives must to be quantifiable so that people may monitor their development and assess their performance in an unbiased manner. With the use of measurable goals, people may keep an eye on their progress, spot areas for development, and change as necessary to stay on track to meet their goals.

3. Achievability: Considering people's skills, resources, and situations, goals should be reasonable and doable. While creating reasonable objectives fosters a sense of confidence and momentum that drives development and success, setting too ambitious or unattainable goals can lead to

dissatisfaction and demotivation.

4. Relevance: Individuals' values, priorities, and aspirations should be taken into consideration when setting goals. Relevance makes ensuring that objectives have purpose and inspires people to persevere in reaching them in the face of difficulties or setbacks.

5. Time-bound: Objectives ought to have distinct due dates and completion milestones. Time-bound goals inspire people to act and move closer to reaching their objectives within a given timeframe by fostering a sense of urgency and accountability.

Techniques for Acting

After objectives are established, obtaining wealth and financial success requires taking action in order to make dreams come true. Action in the millionaire mindset is directed by multiple critical tactics:

1. Divide objectives into doable steps: Divide more ambitious objectives into more achievable, smaller activities and actions that may be completed one at a time. When goals are broken down into smaller steps, people can move forward more quickly and maintain motivation as they strive to accomplish their goals.

2. Make a strategic strategy: Formulate a plan that outlines the precise steps, materials, and deadlines required to fulfill each goal. This can be referred to as a roadmap or strategic plan. A strategic plan offers a precise structure for action, assisting people in maintaining organization and priority focus.

3. Sort duties and tasks into priority lists according to their urgency and relevance. Pay particular attention to high-impact projects that will immediately help you reach

your objectives. People can maximize their productivity and effectiveness by allocating their time and resources wisely and setting effective priorities for their jobs.

4. Be constant in your actions: The millionaire mindset places a premium on consistency. Take consistent, methodical activity toward your objectives, remaining motivated and focused in the face of challenges or disappointments. Over time, consistent activity generates momentum and advancement that provide better outcomes and success.

5. Track development and make necessary course adjustments: Track your progress toward your objectives on a regular basis and objectively assess your outcomes. In order to stay on track to accomplish your goals, be prepared to modify your plan of action and make necessary adjustments if you run into difficulties.

The Millionaire Mindset's Emphasis on Goal-Setting and Action

Setting objectives and taking action are not only tactics for accumulating riches in the millionaire mindset; they are core ideas that guide the entire success philosophy. People can make a success plan and fulfill their financial dreams by establishing clear, defined goals and acting consistently and purposefully to attain them.

In addition, establishing objectives and carrying them out fosters the discipline, concentration, and resolve necessary for success in any undertaking. Through deliberate effort and dedication, they enable people to take charge of their destiny, overcome challenges, and build the life they have always dreamed of.

In the millionaire mindset, goal-setting and action are

crucial components of wealth generation. People can make a strategy for success and reach their financial goals by setting clear, defined goals and putting strategic plans in place to reach them. A life of abundance and fulfillment can be created by those who are committed to advancement and growth, disciplined in their activity, and persistent in their goal-setting. Are you prepared to reach your financial goals by setting high standards and acting decisively? The voyage has begun.

Overcoming Obstacles and Limiting Beliefs in the Millionaire Mindset

One of the biggest problems people encounter in their quest for prosperity and abundance is getting over self-limiting ideas and other barriers that prevent them from reaching their full potential. Under the millionaire mindset, these ideas and challenges are seen as chances for development, education, and personal improvement rather than as insurmountable hurdles. We will dive into the core ideas, tactics, and methods that enable people to overcome self-imposed constraints and realize their objectives in this thorough examination of overcoming limiting beliefs and barriers inside the millionaire mindset.

Knowing What Limiting Beliefs Are

Deeply rooted ideas, attitudes, and perceptions known as limiting beliefs prevent people from realizing their full potential. They might take the form of self-sabotage, fear, insecurity, or self-doubt and are frequently the result of early training, cultural influences, society conventions, and childhood experiences.

Typical instances of limiting beliefs are as follows:

- I'm not sufficiently intelligent to succeed.
- I don't have the potentials to accomplish my goals.
- Being successful is only for lucky people.
- I'll never be able to conquer my financial challenges.

These ideas have a profound effect on people's thoughts, feelings, and actions, which can result in self-limiting patterns and behaviors that impede their success and advancement.

Limiting Beliefs' Effects

Limiting beliefs can have a significant effect on people's life by influencing how they see themselves, their skills, and their potential. They have the power to erect a self-made glass ceiling that keeps people from realizing their dreams and ambitions, regardless of their aptitude or ability. Furthermore, limiting beliefs can result in avoidance tactics, procrastination, and self-sabotage that keep people from taking the required actions to accomplish their goals. They have the power to start a vicious circle of pessimism and negativity that feeds into the notion that success is unattainable.

Overcoming limiting beliefs is viewed in the millionaire mindset as a necessary first step on the road to success and fulfillment. Millionaires know that all greatness starts in the mind and that they can alter their reality and design the life of their dreams by altering their beliefs and perceptions.

Techniques for Dispelling Limiting Thoughts

In order to overcome restricting beliefs, one must make a conscious effort to refute and question unfavorable ideas and impressions. Thankfully, people can employ a number of techniques to get past limiting beliefs and realize their full potential:

1. Determine and confront limiting beliefs: Invest some time in determining the beliefs that are preventing you from reaching your objectives. Examine the facts that either supports or contradicts these ideas in order to cast doubt on their veracity. Positive affirmations and powerful beliefs that support your objectives and desires should take the place of negative self-talk.

2. Use the power of vision to see yourself succeeding and leading the life you have always desired. Envision oneself conquering hindrances, enduring through difficulties, and eventually reaching accomplishment. You may rewire your subconscious mind to believe that you can

accomplish your goals by envisioning success.

3. Take inspired action: Whether it's stepping outside of your comfort zone or facing your worries, overcome analysis paralysis and take inspired action toward your goals. Prioritize progress over perfection and acknowledge and appreciate each little accomplishment as you go. By moving forward, you get momentum and self-assurance that will enable you to go over barriers and restricting ideas.

4. Seek advice and assistance: Be in the company of encouraging, like-minded people who have faith in your abilities. Seek out friends, coaches, or mentors who can provide accountability, support, and direction as you strive to overcome limiting beliefs and accomplish your objectives.

5. Exercise, meditation, and relaxation techniques are examples of self-care practices. Make time for these

activities to take care of your physical, mental, and emotional well-being. Engage in activities that invigorate your body, mind, and spirit and restore your energy reserves, enabling you to remain resilient and concentrated when confronted with obstacles.

6. Step outside of your comfort zone and take on new tasks and experiences that will push you beyond your comfort zone and broaden your horizons. Accept failure as a necessary component of learning and seize the chance to improve and advance from setbacks.

The Millionaire Mindset's Emphasis on Overcoming Limiting Beliefs

Overcoming limiting ideas is not only a personal growth goal, but a must for success and plenty in the billionaire mindset. Millionaires know that all greatness starts in the mind and that they can alter their reality and design the life of their dreams by altering their beliefs and perceptions. Furthermore, invention, originality, and resilience are crucial in the corporate and entrepreneurial worlds where conquering limiting beliefs is crucial. To thrive in today's cutthroat business environment, entrepreneurs need to be able to question the status quo, think creatively, and endure in the face of uncertainty and misfortune. In the millionaire mindset, overcoming limiting beliefs is a crucial first step to success and fulfillment. others can liberate themselves from self-imposed limits and realize their full potential by confronting negative ideas and views, acting with inspiration toward their objectives, and surrounding themselves with encouraging others who share their belief in their abilities. While difficulties and setbacks are unavoidable on the path to achievement, they don't have to determine one's fate. No matter how enormous or intimidating they may seem, people can overcome any obstacle and realize their dreams by developing resilience, tenacity, and a positive mindset. Are you prepared to go past your self-limiting ideas and realize your greatest potential? The voyage has begun.

Developing Persistence and Resilience

Building resilience and tenacity is a key component of the millionaire mindset, as it is in the pursuit of long-term success and fulfillment. These two attributes are critical for overcoming the obstacles, disappointments, and doubts that come with the path to achievement. We will go into the core ideas, tactics, and methods that enable people to overcome challenges and endure in the face of adversity in this in-depth examination of developing resilience and persistence within the billionaire mindset.

Comprehending Persistence and Resilience

Resilience is the capacity to overcome hardships, obstacles, and setbacks with dignity and tenacity. It include cultivating coping skills, adaptable tactics, and an optimistic outlook that help people get through challenging circumstances and come out more resilient and stronger than before. Contrarily, persistence is the unwavering dedication to pursuing objectives and desires in the face of challenges, disappointments, and defeats. It entails having the fortitude to press on in the face of difficulty, to stay focused and determined, and to keep going toward one's goals with unyielding resolution. The cornerstones of the millionaire mindset are perseverance and resilience, which provide people the inner strength, fortitude, and resilience they need to face challenges, weather storms, and achieve long-term fulfillment and achievement.

The Value of Tenacity and Resilience

Resilience and persistence are crucial traits in the pursuit of achievement that set successful people apart from unsuccessful ones. The path to achievement is seldom easy or straight; it is paved with detours and turns, difficulties and disappointments, and unforeseen impediments that can try even the most driven people.

People that possess resilience and tenacity are able to weather these storms, handle ambiguity, and recover from setbacks with newfound vigor and resolve. They give people the inner strength and resilience required to keep going forward in the face of difficulties, remain optimistic in the face of adversity, and remain focused on their goals. Resilience and persistence are also necessary for long-term success maintenance, in addition to being necessary for attaining success. To maintain success and keep developing and adapting, people need to be able to pivot when needed, adjust to new difficulties, and endure in the face of difficulty in the fast-paced, constantly-evolving world of business and entrepreneurship.

Techniques for Developing Persistence and Resilience

It takes deliberate work, practice, and dedication to develop resilience and tenacity. Thankfully, there are a number of techniques people can employ to develop these traits and progressively increase their perseverance and resilience:

1. Develop a growth attitude: Rather than seeing hurdles as

insurmountable, develop a growth mindset that sees challenges and setbacks as chances for learning and growth. Accept failure as a necessary component of the learning process and see setbacks as chances to improve your methods, techniques, and abilities.

2. Practice self-care: Give self-care activities like exercise, mindfulness, meditation, and relaxation techniques top priority in order to take care of your physical, mental, and emotional well-being. Take care of yourself by engaging in activities that boost your energy levels and let you face obstacles head-on and with resilience.

3. Seek assistance and direction: Never hesitate to seek for assistance when you need it. In trying circumstances, seek out the support, direction, and encouragement of friends, family, mentors, or coaches. Embrace a network of people

who are there to support you,
who have faith in your skills,
and who can provide insightful
opinions and new views to
help you overcome obstacles.
4. Establish reasonable
objectives: Divide your
objectives into more doable,
smaller activities and realistic
milestones. Appreciate every
little accomplishment along
the road and use it as
inspiration to keep going in the
direction of your bigger goals.
Even in the face of setbacks,
you may retain momentum and
a sense of progress and
accomplishment by setting
realistic goals and monitoring
your progress.
5. Sustain an optimistic
outlook: Rather than
concentrating on issues or
disappointments, cultivate an
optimistic outlook that
emphasizes possibilities,
chances, and solutions. Strive
for positivity and thankfulness,
see the good in every
circumstance, and take the

opportunity to learn from obstacles and disappointments. 6. Remain flexible and adaptive: Show that you are prepared to modify your plans and strategy in response to unforeseen obstacles or shifting conditions. Remain adaptable and receptive, viewing change as a chance for development and education as opposed to opposing it out of uncertainty or fear.

The Millionaire Mindset's Emphasis on Persistence and Resilience

Resilience and tenacity are not only traits in the millionaire mindset; they are tenets that influence every facet of a person's path to achievement and contentment. Millionaires are aware that hurdles and setbacks are a part of the path to success, but they also know that how one handles these setbacks and challenges will ultimately define their destiny.

Millionaires use failures and losses as stepping stones to greater success and fulfillment, viewing them as chances for personal development and education. They know that achieving success is a journey rather than a destination, and that the keys to traveling that path with poise, tenacity, and optimism are resilience and persistence.

Moreover, perseverance and resilience are necessary traits for long-term success and longevity in the economic and entrepreneurial worlds. To survive and prosper in the long run, people need to be able to adapt, innovate, and persevere in the face of adversity in an environment marked by uncertainty, volatility, and rapid change.

In order to achieve long-term success and fulfillment in the millionaire mindset, it is imperative to cultivate resilience and tenacity. People may overcome challenges, weather adversity's storms, and accomplish their goals with grace and persistence by developing these traits and incorporating them into every part of their lives.

The traits of resilience and persistence enable people to overcome obstacles in their path, keep their resolve and focus, and recover from failures in order to achieve their goals. They provide people the inner fortitude, resilience, and strength they need to face challenges, deal with uncertainty, and realize their goals—which eventually results in a life full of meaning, fulfillment, and purpose. Are you prepared to develop a resilient and persistent life and embrace the secrets of long-term success? The voyage has begun.

The Millionaire Mindset: Capitalizing on Opportunities and

Taking Reasonable Risks

The millionaire mindset involves more than just accumulating wealth in the pursuit of financial success and abundance; it also includes taking a calculated risk-taking strategy and using opportunity detection, leveraging, and capitalization strategies. We will dive into the core ideas, tactics, and methods that millionaires employ to recognize opportunities, weigh risks, and make wise decisions that result in long-term wealth and success in this thorough examination of leveraging opportunities and taking measured risks within the millionaire mindset.

Comprehending the Millionaire Mentality

Believing in the abundance of chances and being prepared to take measured risks in order to capitalize on them are at the heart of the billionaire mindset. Millionaires are aware that success is mostly a product of their ability to see and take advantage of opportunities as they present themselves, as well as to manage risks with courage and resiliency.

A growth-oriented mindset, a proactive strategy to problem-solving, and a readiness to welcome change and ambiguity are traits of the millionaire mindset. Rather than viewing hurdles as insurmountable, millionaires view challenges as chances for learning and progress, and they seize every chance with optimism, curiosity, and resolve.

In addition, taking measured risks to achieve one's objectives and ambitions is a hallmark of the millionaire mindset. Millionaires recognize that taking measured risks is essential to achieving substantial development and success, even while these risks may entail uncertainty and probable setbacks. To reduce risks and increase their chances of success, they perform in-depth study and analysis, balance prospective benefits against potential drawbacks, and create backup plans.

Finding Possibilities

The ability to recognize opportunities in both favorable and adverse circumstances is one of the fundamental tenets of the millionaire mindset. Millionaires are aware that chances don't always present themselves easily and sometimes call for ingenuity, resourcefulness, and an acute sense of potential. Millionaires keep themselves updated about market dynamics, emerging prospects, and industry trends. They proactively seek out novel concepts, investigate uncharted territory, and build a network of associates, mentors, and

advisers who can offer perceptions, counsel, and assistance when the right circumstances emerge.
In addition, millionaires are flexible and open-minded individuals who are prepared to investigate novel concepts, chances, and prospects—even if they diverge from their initial goals or anticipations. They welcome change and uncertainty, knowing that possibilities can arise in ways they hadn't anticipated and necessitating a change in course and strategy.

Evaluation of Risks

Even if they are risk-takers, millionaires do so carefully and strategically. When assessing risks, one must balance the possible benefits against the possible drawbacks and make judgments based on a careful analysis of the information at hand.
To obtain perspectives and insights that guide decision-

making, millionaires interact with mentors or trusted advisors, carry out in-depth study, and compile pertinent data. They create backup plans to deal with unforeseen roadblocks or setbacks and take into account variables including probability, impact, and alternative mitigation techniques.

Additionally, millionaires acknowledge the chance of failure and setback while keeping their attention on the prospective benefits and growth prospects. They are also willing to face their doubts, anxieties, and insecurities. They welcome ambiguity and uncertainty because they understand that taking chances is necessary to achieve success and fulfillment.

Techniques for Capitalizing on Possibilities

Apart from comprehending the tenets of the millionaire

mindset, millionaires employ other pragmatic approaches to capitalize on prospects and optimize their prospects for achievement:

1. Keep yourself educated and vigilant: Millionaires stay up to date on market dynamics, industry trends, and potential new possibilities.

2. Create a network and foster relationships: Millionaires seek to establish a network of contacts, mentors, and advisors who can offer guidance, counsel, and assistance when needed.

3. Be flexible and open-minded: Millionaires like change and uncertainty and are eager to consider novel concepts, chances, and avenues.

4. Act decisively: When possibilities arise, millionaires don't hesitate to act upon them, grasping the chance to advance by taking measured risks.

5. Learn from experience: Millionaires take stock of their prior encounters and apply

lessons learned from both triumphs and setbacks to guide decisions and actions in the future.

Techniques for Taking Reasonably High Risks

Taking calculated risks requires a logical, strategic approach that is marked by thorough planning, analysis, and thought. Millionaires employ a variety of techniques to successfully take measured risks, including:

1. Evaluate the possible advantages and disadvantages of each risk, balancing the possible benefits against the possible drawbacks. Millionaires do this by assessing the potential rewards and consequences.

2. Obtain pertinent facts, knowledge, and insights to guide decision-making through extensive research. When necessary, millionaires carry out feasibility studies, financial analyses, and market research.

3. Create backup plans: Wealthy individuals foresee future hindrances, disappointments, and difficulties and create backup plans to reduce risks and adverse effects.

4. Seek guidance and input: In order to obtain viewpoints and insights that can assist in guiding decision-making and risk assessment, millionaires confer with dependable mentors, advisors, or subject matter experts.

5. Start small and work your way up: Successful people start with little, acceptable risks and work their way up gradually as they acquire expertise and confidence. They also learn from each experience and modify their strategy as necessary.

The Significance of Mentality

A person's attitude, beliefs, and behaviors are greatly influenced by their mindset, which is important when it comes to seizing chances and taking measured risks. It takes a growth mindset to seize opportunities and take measured risks with courage and resiliency. It is defined by the conviction that one can learn, develop, and overcome obstacles.

Moreover, overcoming challenges and disappointments along the road requires a positive mindset that is marked by optimism, perseverance, and a sense of potential.

Getting the Hang of Money Management

One of the main tenets of the millionaire mindset is the ability to manage money well, which is essential to achieving prosperity and financial success. It entails more than just making money; in order to grow wealth and meet long-term financial objectives, it also requires intelligent investing, disciplined saving, and strategic budgeting. We will go into the essential concepts, tactics, and methods that millionaires employ to successfully manage their finances and build long-lasting wealth in this thorough examination of mastering money management within the billionaire mindset.

Comprehending the Millionaire Mentality

Proactive and strategic money management is the cornerstone of the millionaire mindset. Millionaires are aware of how crucial preparation, financial discipline, and foresight are to realizing their dreams and ambitions. They understand that managing and building wealth over time depends more on one's ability to manage resources than it does on income.

Commitment to financial prudence, readiness to make educated judgments, and an emphasis on long-term wealth creation are characteristics of the millionaire mindset. Millionaires place a high value on financial literacy and education, always looking to increase their understanding of topics like investing, saving, and budgeting.

Furthermore, the idea in abundance and possibilities is the foundation of the billionaire mindset. Millionaires know that everyone can become wealthy if they have the correct attitude and work consistently to achieve their financial objectives. They approach money management with self-assurance, hope, and a clear sense of purpose because they understand that with careful financial preparation and execution, they can build the life of their dreams.

The Base of Financial Success: Budgeting

Effective money management starts with budgeting, which offers a road map for allocating income, controlling expenses, and reaching financial objectives. Budgeting is viewed in the millionaire mindset as empowering rather than limiting, allowing people to take charge of their money and deliberately choose how they spend their resources. Millionaires know how important it is to prioritize their spending according to their values and objectives and to live within their means. They develop thorough budgets that take into consideration all sources of income and outlays, including contributions to savings and investments, as well as variable costs like entertainment and food and fixed costs like housing and utilities.

Furthermore, millionaires update and modify their budgets on a regular basis to account for variations in their earnings, outlays, and financial objectives. They keep a careful eye on their expenditures, seeing where they may make savings or reallocate funds to better fit their goals and priorities.

Conserving

A key component of the millionaire mindset's money management strategy is saving, which lays the groundwork for long-term wealth accumulation and monetary stability. Millionaires know how important it is to save regularly and deliberately, allocating a portion of their income for chances, future objectives, and emergencies.
Millionaires consider saving as a non-negotiable expense that comes before discretionary spending, and they demonstrate this by

automating contributions to savings and investing accounts. They build up emergency savings to deal with unforeseen costs and losses, making sure they have a safety net of money in case things go wrong. Additionally, millionaires embrace a delayed gratification mindset, forgoing indulgences and pleasures in the short term in favor of long-term financial freedom and stability. They create savings objectives and benchmarks, acknowledging their accomplishments and utilizing them as inspiration to keep accumulating wealth over time.

Making Investments

In the millionaire mindset, investing is the secret to building money and reaching financial independence. Millionaires know that conserving money is not enough; they also need to invest it in assets that will increase in value over time and provide them with passive income.

Millionaires spread their investments over a range of asset classes, including stocks, bonds, real estate, and business endeavors, with a smart and varied attitude. Before making an investment, they carry out extensive research and due diligence, looking for assets with the highest potential for long-term growth and profitability.

Furthermore, millionaires accept risk as a necessary component of investment since they know that greater rewards are frequently accompanied by higher risk. They choose investments that fit their financial goals, objectives, and risk appetite after carefully evaluating their time horizon and risk tolerance.

Effective Techniques for Becoming an Expert in Money Management

Apart from comprehending the tenets of the millionaire mindset, millionaires employ various pragmatic approaches to proficiently handle their finances:

1. Make a thorough budget by keeping track of your earnings and outlays, allocating spending according to your goals and values, and reviewing and adjusting it on a regular basis.

2. Automate savings and investing: To guarantee consistency and discipline in saving and investing, set up automatic contributions to savings and investment accounts.

3. Make emergency savings a priority. Create an emergency fund with the goal of covering three to six months' worth of living expenses in order to

prepare for unforeseen costs
and setbacks.
4. Invest in a variety of asset
types and investment vehicles
to spread your money around
and reduce risk while
maximizing your potential
rewards.
5. Never stop learning: Keep
up with the latest
developments in personal
finance and investing trends,
tactics, and best practices.
Look for ways to increase your
understanding of and
proficiency with money
management.
6. Seek expert guidance: To
obtain viewpoints and insights
that can guide your financial
strategy and decisions, speak
with mentors, planners, or
financial advisors.
Achieving affluence and long-
term financial success requires
mastering money management.
Effective money management,
according to the millionaire
mindset, entails smart
investing, disciplined saving,
and strategic budgeting in

order to accumulate wealth and meet financial objectives. by taking a proactive, methodical approach to management.

Encircling Yourself with Achievement

The millionaire mindset stresses the value of building valuable connections and surrounding oneself with a network of supportive, like-minded people in addition to individual effort and strategy in the quest of financial wealth and success. We will go into the core ideas, tactics, and methods that millionaires use to create and maintain meaningful connections that support their success and fulfillment in this in-depth examination of the significance of relationships within the millionaire mindset.

Comprehending the Millionaire Mentality

The billionaire mindset is based on the idea that cooperation, synergy, and support from one another may be powerful forces. Millionaires are aware that teamwork, shared insights, and collective understanding frequently lead to success rather than individual accomplishment. They understand the value of forming solid, enduring bonds with people who share their beliefs, objectives, and aspirations.

The proactive strategy to networking, relationship-building, and community involvement is indicative of the millionaire mindset. Millionaires are always looking for ways to meet new people, whether it's at social gatherings, professional associations, networking events, or mentorship programs. They embrace relationships with curiosity, openness, and genuineness, realizing that every connection is an opportunity to develop, learn, and broaden their horizons.

Furthermore, the spirit of plenty, reciprocity, and generosity is the foundation of the billionaire mindset. Millionaires are aware that by providing value, encouragement, and support to others, they foster goodwill and positive energy that can ultimately work to their own advantage. They approach relationships with an abundance mentality, believing that there is more than enough wealth and success for everyone.

Creating Deeply Meaningful Connections

Developing deep connections with others who share their beliefs, objectives, and aspirations is one of the fundamental tenets of the millionaire mindset.

Millionaires are aware of the clear correlation between the caliber of their relationships and their level of fulfillment in both their personal and professional lives.

Building solid, encouraging relationships with people who push, encourage, and inspire them to do greater things is a top priority for millionaires. They look for mentors, counselors, and role models who can offer direction, encouragement, and insight derived from their own accomplishments and experiences.

In addition, millionaires build connections with associates, coworkers, and partners who share their goals and aspirations. This helps them build a network of like-minded people who can provide support, accountability, and encouragement as they pursue their goals. They realize that by being in the company of optimistic, accomplished people, they may take advantage of the opportunities, resources, and collective knowledge to hasten their own development.

The Influence of Coaching and Mentoring

A key element of the millionaire mindset is mentoring and coaching, which offer people on their path to success insightful direction, encouragement, and support. Millionaires look for coaches and mentors who, drawing from their own knowledge and experiences, can provide guidance, support, and insights.

Through mentoring and coaching relationships, people have the exceptional chance to learn from successful experts in their areas, receiving insightful knowledge and practical tactics that will help them better manage hurdles and reach their goals.

Additionally, mentoring and coaching relationships provide people a feeling of structure and direction as they work toward their goals by offering accountability, encouragement, and support. Millionaires know how important it is to surround themselves with mentors and coaches who will push them to grow, force them to step outside of their comfort zones, and hold them responsible for achieving their ambitions.

Creating Connections and Involving the Community

A key component of the millionaire mindset is networking and community involvement, which provide people the chance to meet people, exchange ideas, and work together on initiatives and projects. Millionaires know how important it is to have a wide range of contacts and relationships that can provide insightful information, resources, and chances for personal development.

To broaden their networks and create enduring relationships with peers and colleagues, millionaires engage in professional organizations, industry events, and networking groups. They approach networking with sincerity, authenticity, and a true desire to develop relationships with people that will benefit both parties.

In addition, millionaires give back to the community and advance society through charity and community service. They know that they can have a beneficial impact on their communities and enhance their own sense of fulfillment by devoting their time, efforts, and resources to causes and organizations that they support.

Emotional Intelligence's Function

Within the millionaire mindset, emotional intelligence is a crucial competency that helps people manage relationships successfully, speak persuasively, and establish rapport and trust with others. Millionaires know that developing deep and fruitful relationships requires social skills, empathy, self-control, and self-awareness.

Through introspection on their own attitudes, sentiments, and actions as well as how these affect their relationships with others, millionaires develop self-awareness. By controlling their emotions and impulses, remaining composed under pressure, and reacting rationally as opposed to impulsively, they demonstrate self-regulation.

Additionally, millionaires exhibit empathy by genuinely caring about the opinions and feelings of others, as well as by comprehending and appreciating those viewpoints and feelings. By speaking clearly, listening intently, and establishing a connection with people, they cultivate strong social skills and produce an atmosphere of cooperation and trust that promotes success and fulfillment.

Realistic Techniques for Establishing Connections

Apart from comprehending the tenets of the millionaire mindset, there exist many pragmatic approaches that folks can use to proficiently establish and maintain significant connections:

1. Be real and authentic: Be yourself in all of your interactions with other people and pursue relationships with sincerity, honesty, and authenticity.

2. Actively and sympathetically listen: Engage in active listening and show

empathy by acknowledging and appreciating the thoughts and emotions of others.

3. Express gratitude and appreciation: Thank people for their contributions and support, and acknowledge their hard work and accomplishments.

4. Be proactive and receptive: Show initiative in establishing and preserving connections, and show consideration for the wants and worries of others.

5. Give value and support: Look for ways to make a good difference in the lives of those around you. Give value, support, and help to others without asking anything in return.

6. Be inclusive and open-minded: Welcome the chance to learn from others who may have different experiences and viewpoints, and be receptive to meeting new people from a variety of backgrounds and viewpoints.

7. Establish a culture of cooperation and teamwork by fostering an atmosphere of

mutual respect, trust, and cooperation that promotes candid conversations, idea exchanges, and cooperation between coworkers.
It is impossible to exaggerate the significance of relationships in the millionaire mindset. Millionaires can more successfully harness the power of cooperation, synergy, and mutual support to achieve their objectives by surrounding themselves with like-minded, helpful people. For success and fulfillment in both personal and professional life, developing meaningful relationships is crucial, whether through networking, coaching, mentoring, or community involvement. Are you prepared to build a network of dependable connections that will enable you to realize your ambitions? The voyage has begun.

Returning the Favor

The millionaire mindset embraces the values of charity and philanthropy in addition to personal gain in the chase of financial success and wealth. Millionaires are aware of the value of contributing to organizations they support, giving back to their communities, and having a positive influence on the world. We will dive into the core ideas, tactics, and methods that millionaires use to give back and effect long-lasting change in their communities and beyond in this in-depth examination of the role of giving and philanthropy within the millionaire mindset.

Comprehending the Millionaire Mentality

The millionaire mindset is based on the ideas of abundance, thankfulness, and compassion. Millionaires are aware that true wealth is not only determined by one's financial situation but also by their legacy and the difference they make in other people's lives. They understand that investing in the well-being of others is not merely a calculated risk but also a moral obligation.

The determination to change the world—whether via monetary gifts, unpaid labor, or advocacy work—is what defines the millionaire mindset. Millionaires know that in addition to improving other people's lives, giving back to the community helps them feel more fulfilled, purposeful, and meaningful themselves.

In addition, the millionaire mindset is based on a sense of social duty, empathy, and charity. Millionaires recognize that they are fortunate to have access to resources and opportunities, and they have a strong sense of responsibility to use their riches and power to improve the lives of others.

The Significance of Charity and Generosity

A key component of the millionaire mindset is generosity and philanthropy, which offer chances for people to support causes they care about, give back to their communities, and positively impact the lives of others. Millionaires are aware that they may have a positive impact and leave a long-lasting legacy of kindness and compassion by giving away their resources, time, and abilities to those in need.
In addition to giving people a sense of fulfillment and purpose, generosity and charity enable people to live out their principles and have a significant impact on the world. Millionaires who give back feel a sense of contentment, joy, and happiness that transcends

worldly prosperity and achievement.

Furthermore, kindness and philanthropy spread like wildfire, encouraging others to do the same and fostering a giving culture in local communities and society at large. Millionaires know that by setting a good example and highlighting the value of kindness and philanthropy, they may encourage others to follow suit and start a beneficial feedback loop.

Methods for Contributing Back

Apart from comprehending the tenets of the billionaire mindset, there exist other pragmatic approaches that individuals might employ to contribute efficiently:

1. Determine the causes and organizations that you are enthusiastic about: Give your values, interests, and passions some thought. Then, find the causes and organizations that

support your objectives and values.

2. Establish giving goals and objectives: Whether your goal is to donate a set portion of your income to charity, volunteer a certain number of hours each month, or support particular initiatives or projects, make sure your philanthropic activities have clear goals and objectives.

3. Research and veterinary organizations: Before donating money or offering your time as a volunteer, spend some time learning about and researching veterinary organizations. Seek out groups that share your beliefs and objectives and have a history of influence, accountability, and transparency.

4. Become active and make an impact: Look for opportunities to become involved and have an impact on your neighborhood and beyond, whether it be through advocacy work, financial contributions, or volunteer

labor. Every donation matters, whether it's made in the form of cash to a nearby charity, time spent volunteering at a homeless shelter, or support of social justice causes.

5. Work together and make the most of your resources: Join forces with other people, groups, and companies to increase your influence and together make a greater difference. You can accomplish more and bring about long-lasting change in your neighborhood and beyond by working together and pooling your resources.

The Effects of Returning the Favor

Giving back has a significant effect on communities and individuals alike, bringing about long-lasting transformation and practical advantages. providing back to others improves people's general well-being and happiness by providing them a feeling of fulfillment, purpose, and meaning. Additionally, it deepens their comprehension of the world around them and reinforces their sense of connectedness to others. Giving back to the community supports vulnerable populations, tackles urgent social concerns, and opens doors for progress. It improves resilience, social cohesiveness, and a feeling of pride in one's community. Giving back also improves a community's general health and vibrancy, which makes society more sustainable and equitable for all.

The Heritage of Charity and Generosity

Giving and philanthropy are not only deeds of compassion in the millionaire mindset; they are a legacy that people leave for the next generation. Giving back to the community enables millionaires to make a positive impact on countless lives and improve the planet much beyond their own lifetimes. Furthermore, the example of philanthropy and generosity encourages others to follow in their footsteps, fostering a culture of giving and service that goes beyond individual deeds and becomes a defining characteristic of society at large. Millionaires establish a lasting legacy that goes far beyond their own success and financial fortune by setting an example and highlighting the value of giving back.

It is impossible to overestimate the significance of philanthropy and generosity in the billionaire mindset. Millionaires who give back leave a lasting legacy of influence, empathy, and social responsibility that goes well beyond their personal wealth. Giving back is an essential part of the millionaire mindset, offering chances for people to change the world and leave a compassionate and generous legacy, whether through monetary donations, volunteer labor, or advocacy campaigns. Are you prepared to change the world around you and embrace the power of philanthropy and generosity? The voyage has begun.

Conclusion

It's important to consider the major ideas, tactics, and realizations that have been covered during this investigation of the billionaire mindset as we draw to a close. The millionaire mindset enables people to design the life of their dreams by adopting a mindset of plenty, fulfillment, and purpose rather than focusing only on gaining wealth. The main conclusions from our conversation will be outlined in this last piece, which will also look at how adopting the millionaire mindset might result in a life that is genuinely meaningful.

Essential Elements of the Millionaire Mentality

The key ideas that underpin the millionaire mindset and direct people toward fulfillment and success are as follows:

1. Adopt an attitude of abundance rather than scarcity, seeing the world to be full of boundless possibilities for development, achievement, and contentment.

2. Develop a growth mindset by viewing obstacles as chances for learning and development rather than as things to be avoided or feared.

3. Purpose-driven action: Focus on worthwhile goals and objectives that provide a sense of satisfaction and fulfillment. Align your actions with your beliefs, interests, and purpose.

4. Strategic thinking: Use your resources, abilities, and experiences to your advantage to accomplish your objectives more successfully. Approach

opportunities and obstacles
with a strategic attitude.
5. Develop your resilience and
determination to get over
setbacks and roadblocks and to
remain dedicated to your
objectives in the face of
hardship.

Methods for Adopting a Millionaire Mentality

Apart from comprehending the
fundamental ideas of the
millionaire mindset, there exist
other pragmatic approaches
that people can employ to
adopt this mindset and
establish a satisfying
existence:
1. Establish measurable goals
and objectives that are in line
with your beliefs, interests, and
purpose. Also, clearly define
your vision for success.
2. Take calculated chances:
Recognize that growth and
achievement frequently call for
bravery and audacity, therefore
be willing to venture beyond
of where you feel at ease and

take calculated risks in pursuit of your objectives and dreams.
3. Learn to handle your money well. To accumulate wealth and become financially independent over time, establish good financial practices such as investing, saving, and budgeting.
4. Build lasting relationships by surrounding yourself with people who share your values and who encourage, inspire, and push you to realize your greatest potential.
5. Give back: Develop a legacy of compassion and influence that goes well beyond your own life by supporting causes you believe in and giving back to your community. This is a kind and philanthropic way to live.

Having a Fulfilling Life by Adopting the Millionaire Mindset

People who adopt the millionaire mindset can design a life that is abundant in fulfillment, meaning, and purpose. They pursue objectives and desires that are in line with their beliefs and passions, focusing on what really matters to them instead of going after financial prosperity or external approval.

Furthermore, by understanding that every problem presents a chance for development and learning, people with a millionaire mindset are better equipped to face setbacks and barriers with perseverance and resilience. They welcome change and uncertainty as chances for both professional and personal growth, and they approach life with a spirit of possibility, wonder, and optimism.

The millionaire attitude also promotes plenty and thankfulness, helping us to appreciate the possibilities and blessings we encounter every day. Regardless of their financial status or outside circumstances, people can feel more joy, fullness, and satisfaction in their life by developing an attitude of thankfulness.

In summary, adopting a billionaire mindset involves building a life that is rich in fulfillment, meaning, and purpose rather than merely amassing fortune. People can realize their greatest potential and design a life that is genuinely meaningful on all levels by embracing the fundamental ideas and techniques discussed in this investigation. Are you prepared to live the life of your dreams and adopt the mindset of a millionaire? The voyage has begun.

www.ingramcontent.com/pod-product-compliance
Lightning Source LLC
Chambersburg PA
CBHW050042260726
48658CB00005B/1736